Corona Pirates
Coloring, & Activity Book

Words by Alexandra McDougall
Illustrations by Robert Demetrio

This book belongs to

a PIRATE
if there ever was one

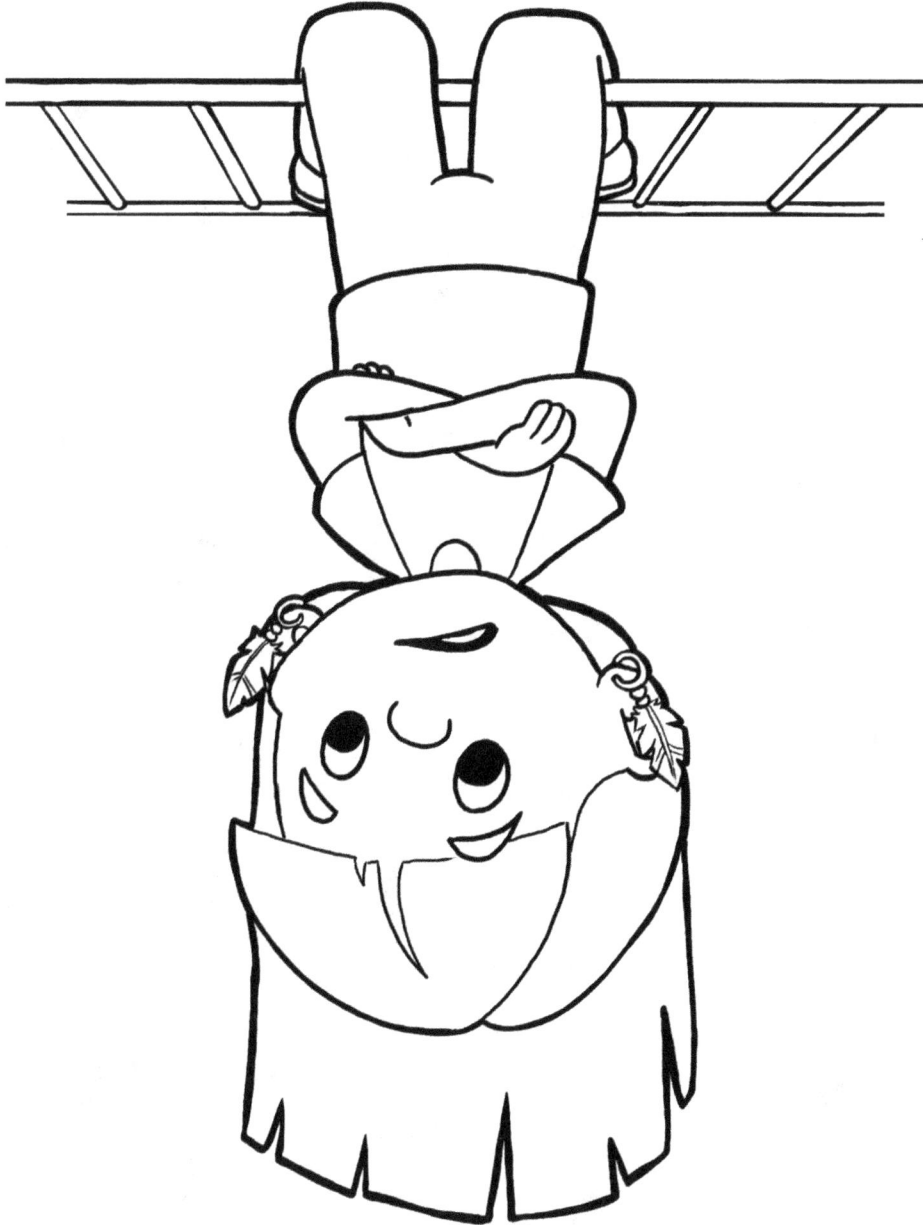

Some Days Are Rough

Draw a line to connect all of the round peanut butter balls.

Making G.G.'s Peanut Butter Balls

Which two are not the same as the others?

Hen-demonium

Follow the directions to make your own newspaper pirate hat.

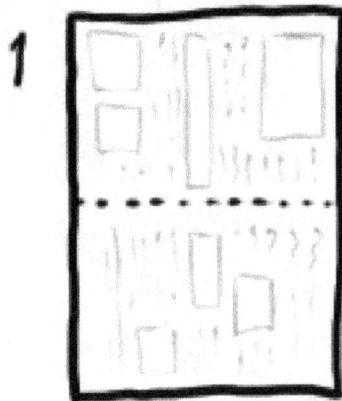

1

Start with a piece of newspaper.

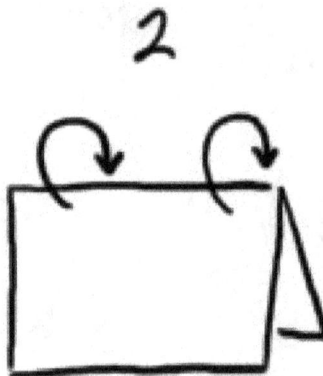

2

Fold the paper in half.

3

Fold the top corners down towards the center of the page.

4

Your paper should look like this.

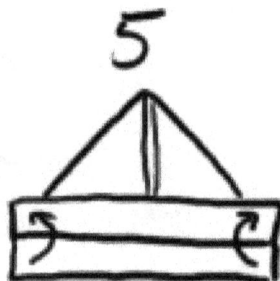

5

Lift the bottom flap, and fold it up.

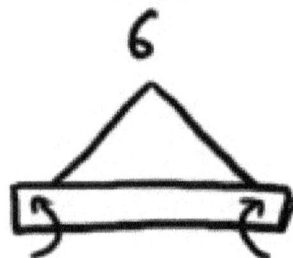

6

Flip the paper over, then fold the bottom flap up.

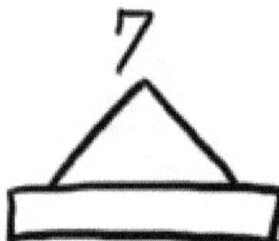

7

Your pirate hat is ready to wear!

Faster! We Need To Ketch-up!

Color the ship by numbers

1. Dark Brown
2. Light Blue
3. Green
4. Tan
5. Dark Blue
6. Yellow
7. Orange
8. Red
9. Purple
10. Gray

Sailing the Bubbly Seas

Turn these circles into anything you choose!

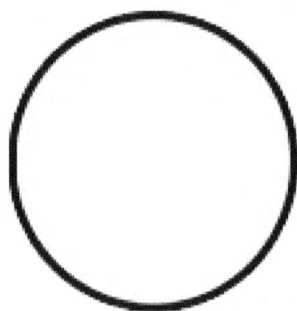

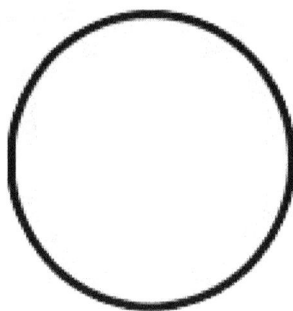

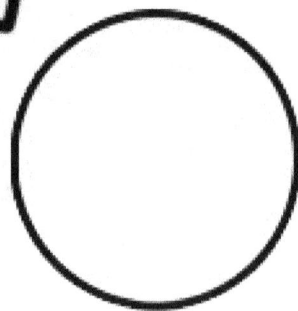

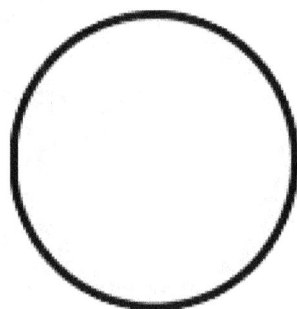

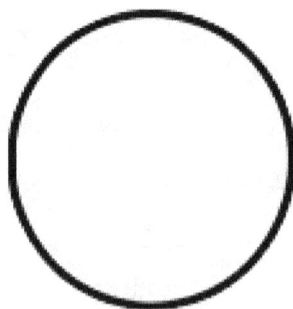

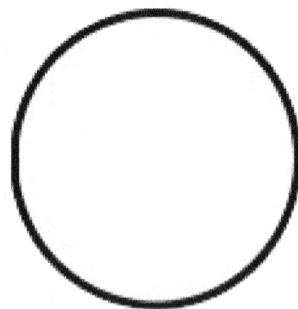

Accidental Flour Angels

Design your own pirate mask!

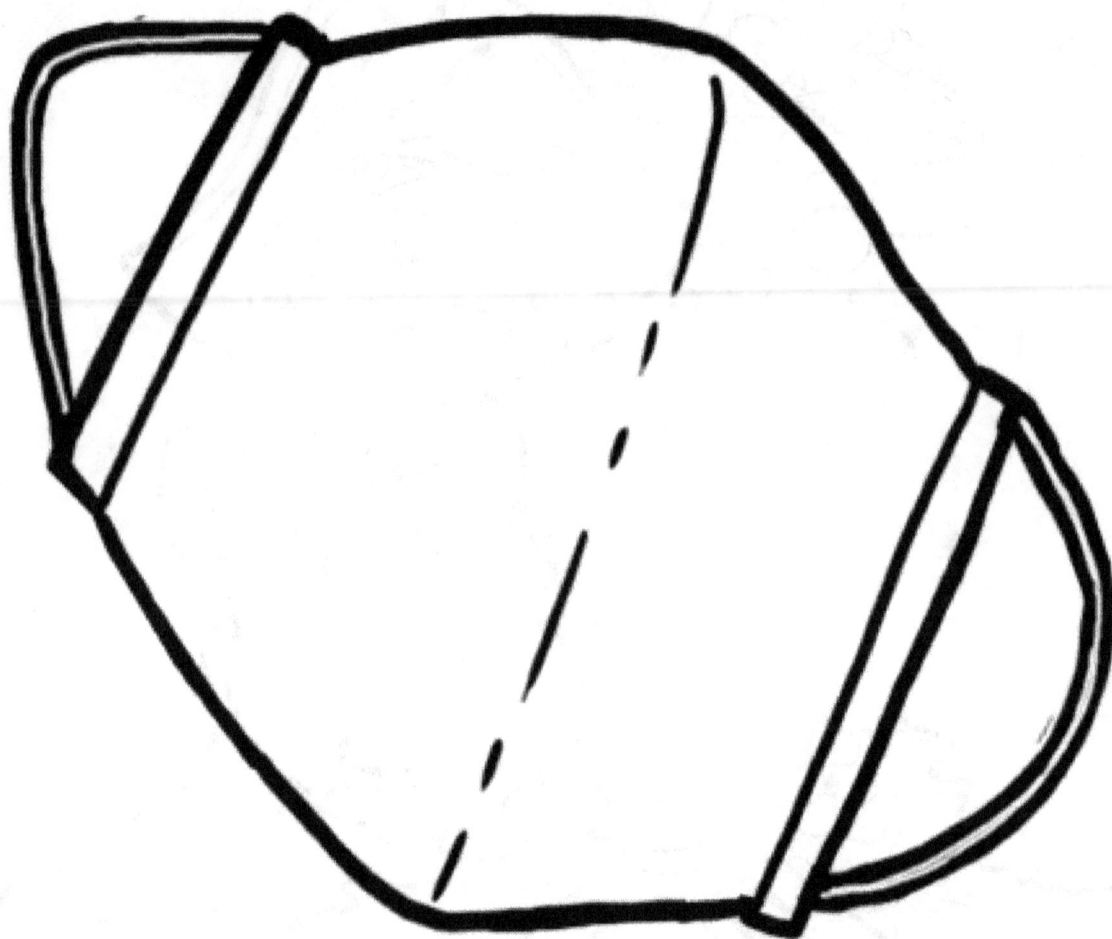

D.I.Y. Masks

Who crossed the finish line?

FINISH LINE

Let the Good Times Roll

How to draw a muffin.

1

2

3

4

5

6

Mmmm, Muffins!

Color in how many bottles of water you drink in a day.

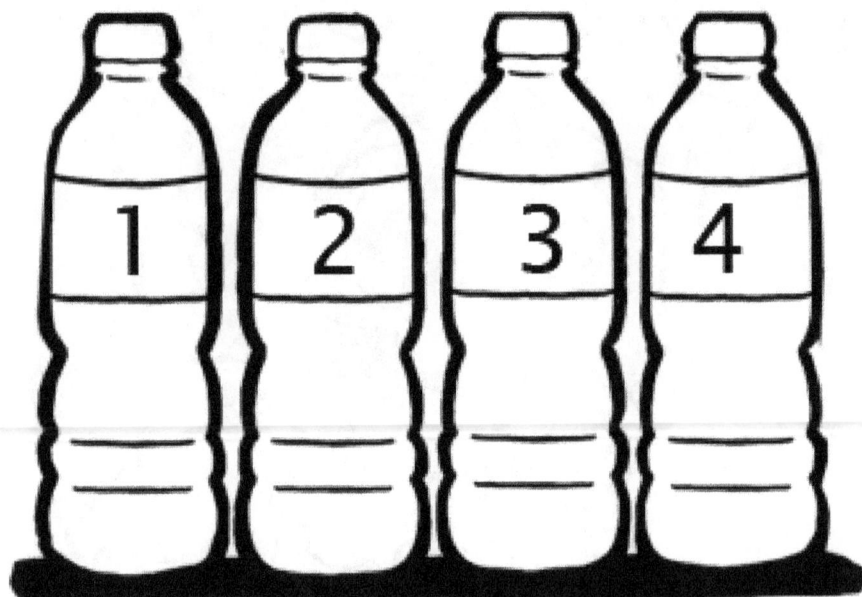

1   2   3   4

6   7   8   9

Water You Doing?

Add your favorite pizza toppings.

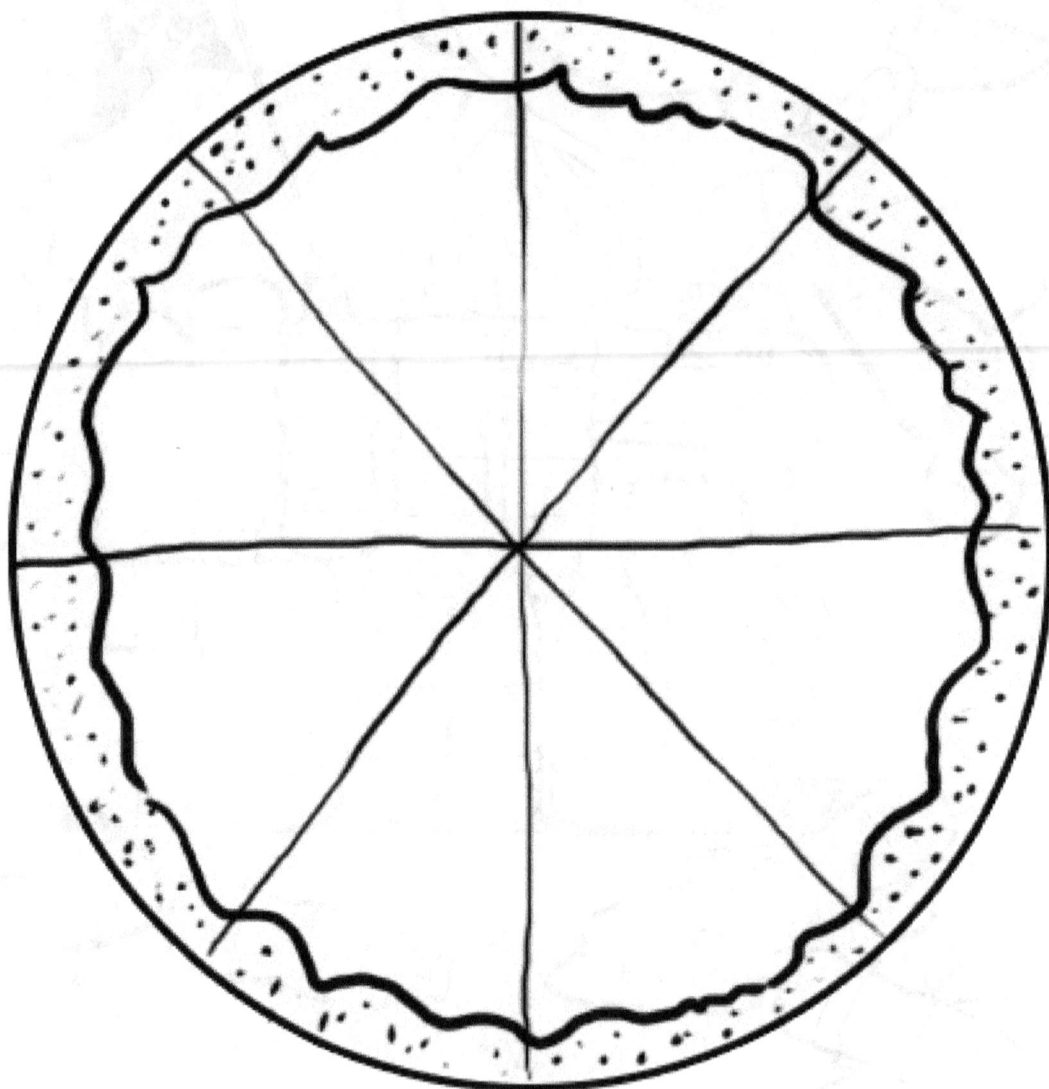

Shiver Me Timbrrrrs!

Make your way through the maze to the finish.

Start

Finish

Snack Mask

Connect the animal to its related item.

Bribing Sir Fluffakins with Tuna

Connect the dots.

You Have Goat To Be Kidding

Name that food.

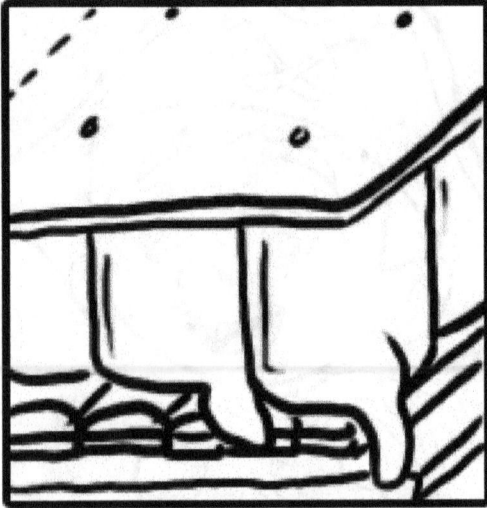

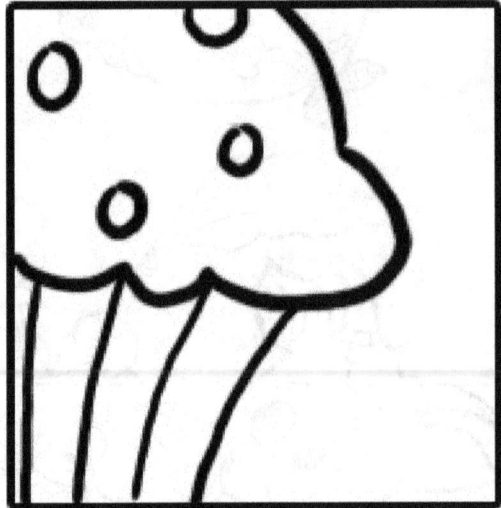

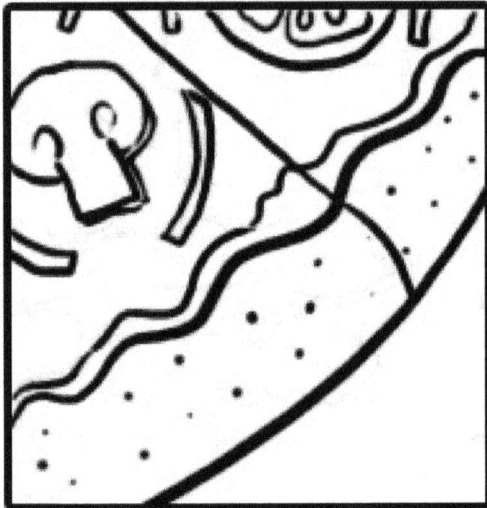

The S'more The Merrier

Make your own treasure map.

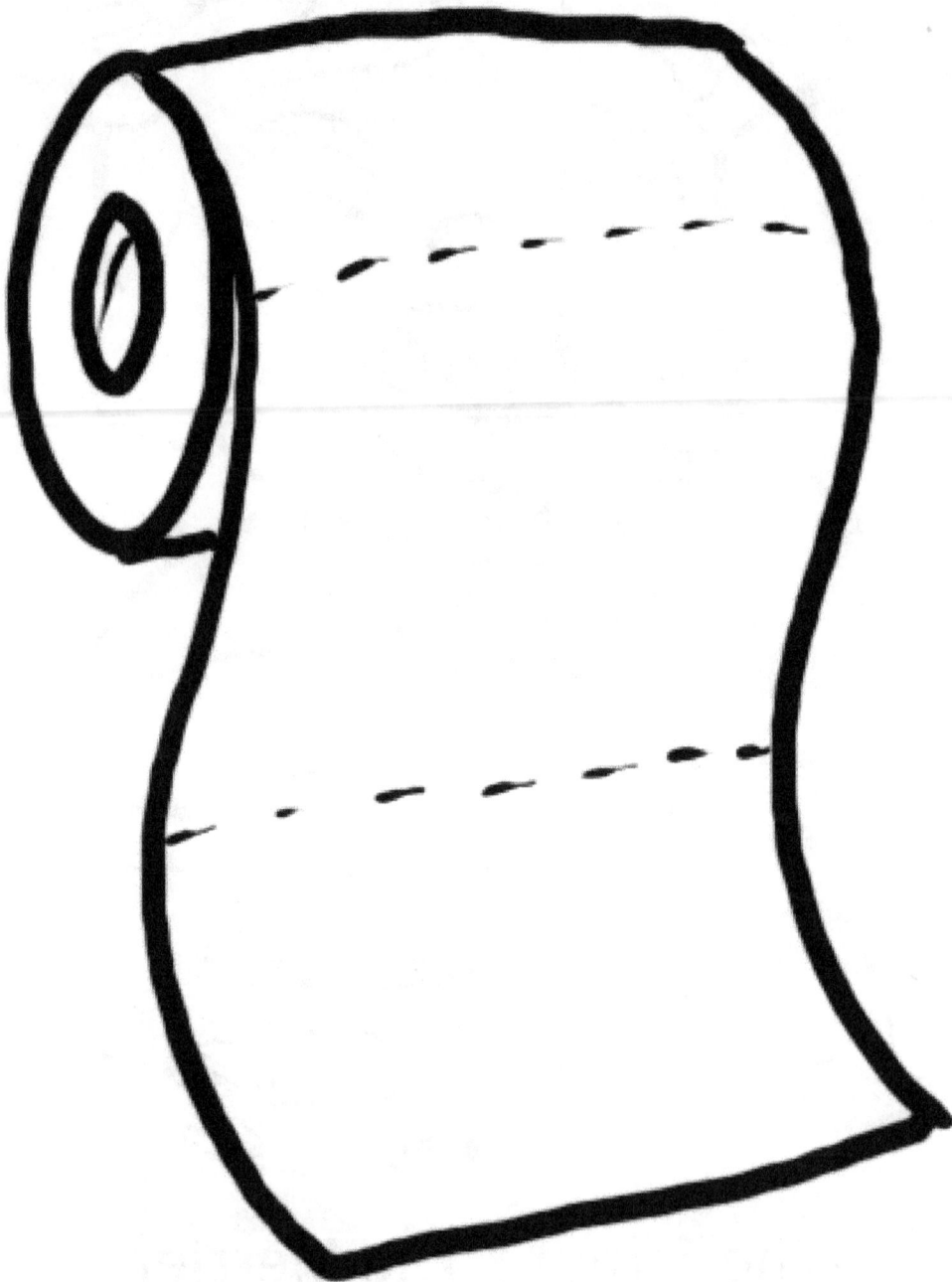

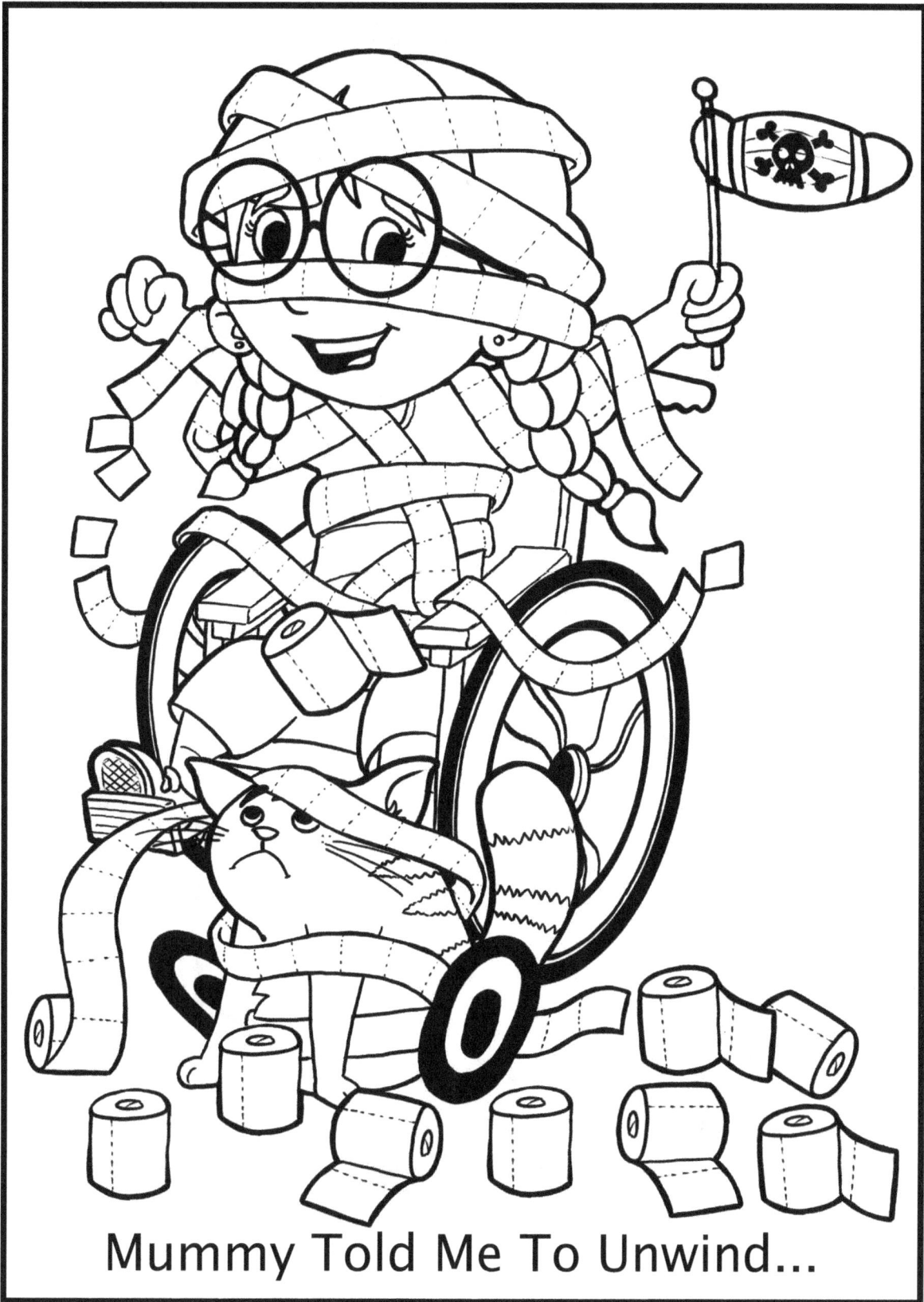

Mummy Told Me To Unwind...

Draw your favorite vegetable, on the can.

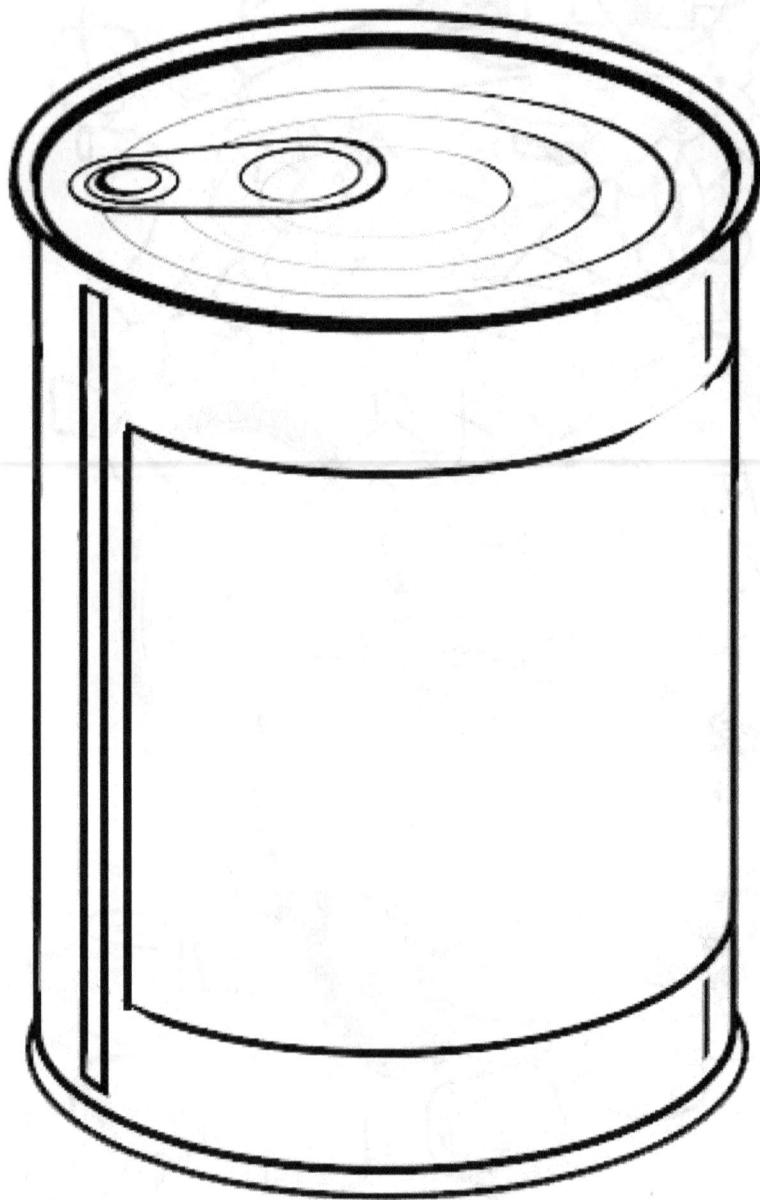

Seemingly Im-mooo-vable